HEREFORDSHIRE
Wit & Humour

LEO GOODRICH

BRADWELL
BOOKS

Published by Bradwell Books

9 Orgreave Close Sheffield S13 9NP

Email: books@bradwellbooks.co.uk

Compiled by Leo Goodrich

British Library Cataloguing in Publication Data: a catalogue record for this book is available from the British Library.

1st Edition

ISBN: 9781910551066

Print: Gomer Press, Llandysul, Ceredigion SA44 4JL

Design by: jenksdesign@yahoo.co.uk/07506 471162

Illustrations: ©Tim O'Brien 2014

The magistrate at Hereford County Court spoke sharply to the defendant, "But if you saw the lady driving towards you, why didn't you give her half the road?"

"I was going to, your Honour," replied the motorist, "…as soon as I could work out which half she wanted."

Q: Why was the woman arrested on a dairy farm in Staunton-on-Wye for wearing a silk dress?

A: She was charged with rustling.

A teacher at a school in Leominster was having a little trouble getting her Year 11 pupils to understand grammar. "These are what we call the pronouns," she said, "We use them with verbs like this: I am, you are, he/she is." The pupils looked at her with glazed expressions.

Trying a different tack, she said, "Lauren, give me a sentence with the pronoun, 'I' in it."

Lauren began, "I is…"

"No, no, no, no, no NO, NO!" shouted the teacher, "Never, 'I is', always, 'I am'… now try again."

Lauren looked puzzled and a little hurt, thought a while then began again more quietly, "I… am…the ninth letter of the alphabet."

Two elderly ladies in Bartestree had been friends for many decades. Over the years, they had shared all kinds of fun but of late their activities had been limited to meeting a few times a week to play cards. One day, they were playing pontoon when one looked at the other and said, "Now don't get mad at me, duck. I know we've been friends for a long time but I just can't think of your name. I've thought and thought, but I can't remember it. Please tell me what your name is." Her friend got a bit cross and, for at least three minutes, she just stared and glared at her. Finally she said, "How soon do you need to know?"

How do you get a sweet old Herefordshire granny to swear? Get another sweet old Herefordshire granny to shout "BINGO!"

Two rival cricketers from Colwall and Marden were having a chat.

"The local team wants me to play for them very badly," said the man from Marden.

"Well," said his friend, "You're just the man for the job."

Q: What did one ocean say to the other ocean?
A: Nothing, they just waved.

Simon was down on his luck so he thought he would try getting a few odd jobs by calling at the posh Georgian houses in Ledbury. After a few "no ways", a guy in one of the big houses thought he would give him a break and says, "The porch needs painting so I'll give you £50 to paint it for me."

"You're life-saver, mister," says Simon, "I'll get started right away!" Time passes until…

"There you go, I'm all done with the painting."

"Well, here's your £50," says the homeowner, handing over some crisp tenners.

"Thanks very much," says Simon, pocketing the money, "Oh and by the way, it's a Ferrari, not a Porsche!"

A lady from London and her friend were on the train going to Leominster when she noticed some Hereford cows in a field.

"What a cute bunch of cows!" she remarked.

"Not a bunch," replied her friend who, as a local woman, knew the collective noun, "herd."

"Heard of what?" said the Londoner.

"Herd of cows," said her friend patiently.

"Of course, I've heard of cows," snapped the city girl.

The Herefordshire lady took a deep breath. "No, a cow herd."

"What do I care if a cow heard?" exclaimed her friend, "I've got nothing to hide…"

Just before the big race at Hereford, the trainer was giving last minute instructions to the jockey and appeared to slip something into the horse's mouth just as a steward walked by. "What was that?" inquired the steward.

"Oh nothing," said the trainer, "just a polo."

He offered one to the steward and had one himself. After the suspicious steward had left the scene, the trainer continued with his instructions.

"Just keep on the rail. You're on a dead cert. The only thing that could possibly pass you down the home straight is either the steward or me".

In the village of Much Dewchurch a couple are bickering…

Wife:"I'm telling you, there's trouble with the car. It has water in the injector."

Husband:"Water in the injector? That's ridiculous."

Wife:"I tell you the car has water in the injector."

Husband:"You don't even know what an injector is. I'll check it out. Where's the car?"

Wife:"In the village pond."

A Hereford United fan was watching his team play in a packed Edgar Street stadium. There was only one empty seat - right next to him.

"Who does that seat belong to?" asked Dave from the row behind.

"I got the ticket for my wife," replied the Bulls fan.
"But why isn't she here?"

"I'm afraid she died in a tragic accident."
"So you're keeping the seat vacant as a mark of respect," said Dave.

"No," said the Bulls fan, "I offered it to all of my friends."
"Then why didn't they take it?" asked a puzzled Dave.
"They've all gone to the funeral."

A lawyer from Cheltenham and a businessman from Hereford ended up sitting next to each other on a long-haul flight.

The lawyer started thinking that he could have some fun at the man from Hereford's expense and asked him if he'd like to play a fun game. The businessman was tired and just wanted to relax. He politely declined the offer and tried to sleep. The lawyer persisted, explaining, "I ask you a question, and if you don't know the answer, you pay me just £5; you ask me one, and if I don't know the answer, I will pay you £500."

This got the businessman a little more interested and he finally agreed to play the game.

The lawyer asked the first question, "What's the distance from the Earth to the moon?"

The man from Hereford said nothing, but reached into his pocket, pulled out a five-pound note and handed it to the lawyer.

Now, it was his turn to ask a question. He asked the lawyer, "What goes up a hill with three legs, and comes down with four?"

The lawyer scratched his head. He looked the question up on his laptop and searched the web. He sent emails to his most well-read friends. He used the air-phone to call his colleagues in Cheltenham, but he still came up with nothing. After over an hour of searching, he finally gave up.

He woke up the businessman and handed him £500. The man pocketed the cash smugly and dozed off again.

The lawyer was wild with curiosity and wanted to know the answer. He shook the businessman awake. "Well? What goes up a hill with three legs and comes down with four?" he demanded.

The businessman reached into his pocket, handed the lawyer £5 and went straight back to sleep.

Derek and Duncan were long-time neighbours in Hoarwithy. Every time, Derek saw Duncan coming round to his house, his heart sank. This was because he knew that, as always, Duncan would be visiting him in order to borrow something and he was fed up with it.

"I'm not going to let Duncan get away with it this time," he said quietly to his wife, "Watch what I'm about to do."

"Hi there, I wondered if you were thinking about using your hedge trimmer this afternoon?" asked Duncan.

"Oh, I'm very sorry," said Derek, trying to look apologetic, "but I'm actually going to be using it all afternoon."

"In that case," replied Duncan with a big grin, "You won't be using your golf clubs, will you? Mind if I borrow them?"

An elderly couple from Eaton Bishop are sitting at the dining table in their semi-detached house talking about making preparations for writing their wills. Bill says to his missus, Edna, "I've been thinking, dear, if I go first to meet me maker I don't want you to be on your own for too long. In fact, I think you could do worse than marry Colin in the Chemists or Dave with the fruit stall in the market. They'd provide for you and look after you when I'm gone."

"That's very kind on you to think about me like that, Bill," replied Edna, "But I've already made my own arrangements!"

A girl from Madley who had just started her first term at Cheltenham Ladies College asked a prefect, "Can you tell me where the library's at?"

The older student said disdainfully, "At Cheltenham Ladies College we never end a sentence with a preposition." The new girl tried again, "Can you tell me where the library's at, you stuck up moo?"

A man from Leominster said to his wife, "Get your coat on, love. I'm off to the club."

His wife said, "That's nice. You haven't taken me out for years." He said, "You're not coming with me...I'm turning the heating off when I go out."

Two elderly ladies were enjoying a small sherry in their local in Wormelow Tump.

One said to the other, "Was it love at first sight when you met your late husband?"

"No, I don't think so," came the reply, "I didn't know how much money he had when I first met him!"

A bloke from Credenhill goes into an artist's studio and asks if the artist could paint a picture of him surrounded by beautiful, scantily clad women. The artist agrees but he is intrigued by this strange request. He asks his new client why he wants such a picture painted and the bloke says, "Well, if I die before me missus when she finds this painting she'll wonder which one I spent all me money on!"

The next day the bloke's wife goes into the artist's studio and asks him to paint her wearing a big diamond necklace and matching earrings.

"Of course, madam," says the artist, "but may I ask why?"
"Well," replies the woman, "if I die before me husband I want his new woman to be frantic searching for all me jewellery!"

Fred's wife has been missing for over a week. The police liaison officer warned him to prepare for the worst…so Fred went to the charity shop to get all her clothes back.

Q: What's the difference between a new husband and a new dog?

A: After a year, the dog is still excited to see you.

What do you get if you cross Gloucester City F.C. with an OXO cube?

A laughing stock.

A Herefordshire man is driving through Gloucestershire when he passes a farmer standing in the middle of a huge field. He pulls the car over and watches the farmer standing stock-still, doing absolutely nothing. Intrigued, the man walks over to the farmer and asks him, "Excuse me sir, but what are you doing?"

The farmer replies, "I'm trying to win a Nobel Prize."

"How?" Asks the puzzled Herefordshire man.

"Well," says the farmer, "I heard they give the prize to people who are outstanding in their field."

A well-known academic from the University of Gloucestershire was giving a lecture on the philosophy of language at Hereford College of Arts. He came to a curious aspect of English grammar.

"You will note," said the somewhat stuffy scholar, "That in the English language, two negatives can mean a positive, but it is never the case that two positives can mean a negative."

To which someone at the back responded, "Yeah, yeah."

Four fonts walk into a bar. The barman says, "Oi - get out! We don't want your type in here"

A police officer was patrolling the lanes outside Kington one night, when he noticed a car swerving all over the road. Quickly, he turned on his lights and siren and pulled the driver over. "Sir, do you know you're all over the road? Please step out of the car."

When the man got out of the car, the policeman told him to walk in a straight line.

"I'd be happy to, offisher," said the drunk, "If you can just get the line to stop moving about."

A man walks into a pub in Little Dewchurch with a roll of tarmac under his arm and says, "Pint please, and one for the road."

A lady works in Hereford and everyday she walks past a pet shop there. One day she notices a parrot in the window and stops to admire the bird. The parrot says to her, "Hallo, darling, you've got a right ugly mush."

Well, the lady is furious! She storms off but, on her way back from work, she passes the same parrot and, when it sees her, the bird says, "Hallo, darling, you've got a right ugly mush."

She is incredibly angry now so she goes to the manager and threatens to sue the pet shop. She demands to have the bird put down. The manager apologises profusely and promises that the bird won't say it again. The next day, she decides to go back and check. She walks past the parrot and, when it sees her, it says, "Hallo, darling."

The woman stops, scowls and with an icy stare, says, "Yes?" The parrot struts back and forth on its perch in a cocky manner gawping at her, then it says, "You know."

At a cricket match in Brockampton, a fast bowler sent one down and it just clipped the bail. As nobody yelled "Ow's att", the batsman picked up the bail and replaced it. He looked at the umpire and said, "Windy today, ain't it?"

"Yes," said the umpire, "Mind it doesn't blow your cap off when you're walking back to the pavilion."

A policeman stops a drunk wandering the streets of Bromyard at four in the morning and says, "Can you explain why you are out at this hour, sir?"

The drunk replies, "If I was able to explain myself, I would have been home with the wife ages ago."

Over a candlelit dinner in Ledbury, Susan's boyfriend, a Gloucestershire lad, proposed marriage to her. "I love the simple things in life," she said with a smile, "but I don't want one of them for my husband."

A DEFRA Inspector goes to a small farm near Ross-on-Wye and knocks the door of the humble, tied cottage. A young boy opens the door and asks what business the man has on his parent's property.

"I've come to inspect the farm for compliance with EU regulations, my boy. Where's your father?"

"You can't speak to him, he's busy," says the surly child.

"I shall speak to him. He's had notice of my visit," the Inspector retorted firmly.

"Well, he's feeding the pigs at the moment, "says the boy, "But you'll be able to tell me father easy enough - he's the one wearing a hat!"

One freezing cold December day, two blondes went for a walk in the Forest of Dean in search of the perfect Christmas tree. Finally, after five hours looking, one turns to the other and says crossly, "That's it, I've had enough. I'm chopping down the next fir tree we see, whether it's decorated or not!"

A reporter from the Hereford Times was covering the local football league and went to see Fownhope F.C. versus Pegasus Reserves F. C. One of the Fownhope players looked so old, he went over to him and said, "You know you might be the oldest man playing in the league. How do you do it at your age?"

The man replied, "I drink six pints of cider every night, smoke two packets of fags a day, and eat loads of chips."

"Wow, that is incredible!" said the reporter, "How old did you say you were?"

"Twenty-two," said the player proudly.

A Much Marcle couple, Enid and Sidney, are having matrimonial difficulties and seek the advice of a counsellor. The couple are shown into a room where the counsellor asks Enid what problems, in her opinion, she faces in her relationship with Sidney.

"Well," she starts, "he shows me no affection, I don't seem to be important to him anymore. We don't share the same interests and I don't think he loves me at all." Enid has tears in her eyes as the counsellor walks over to her, gives her a big hug and kisses her firmly on the lips.

Sidney looks on in passive disbelief. The counsellor turns to Sidney and says, "This is what Enid needs once a day for the next month. Can you see that she gets it?"

Sidney looks unsettled, "Well I can drop her off everyday other than Wednesdays when I play snooker and Sundays when I go fishing!"

A farmer in Monkland says to his friend, "I can't decide whether to buy a bicycle or a new cow."

His friend replies, "You'd look pretty silly riding a cow."

"I'd look even sillier trying to milk a bicycle," retorts the farmer.

Two cows are in a field. One goes: "Moooooo!"
The other cow turns to her: "I was just going to say that."

The Leominster Hockey Club team are having a bad season. One day the team coach has an idea to advertise for a star player, so he places an ad in the Hereford Times.

A few weeks go by and no replies. Then one wet afternoon there's a knock on the clubhouse door... And in walks this horse and says, "Hello, coach, I see you're after a new hockey player?" "Yes," says the surprised coach.

"I'm very good, great ball control, and superb passing skills. All in all, I'm a brilliant team player," says the horse.

"Is that so?" says the coach, thinking here's nothing in the rules that says a horse can't play for the team and he can't be any worst than some of the current players. "You're hired, and you play this weekend."

So, the day arrives and the Leominster Hockey Club lines up for its first game with a horse at centre-half. The game starts slowly and the horse doesn't move much, but when he gets the ball he's able to go round people and change the game.

Eventually, the horse gets the ball on the half-way line, tries his luck and scores.

After the game the horse was relaxing with a nice G&T in the bar and a team-mate came up to congratulate him on winning the game for the team.

"But why don't you run?" asked the player
"RUN!" Thundered the horse, "RUN! My dear chap, if I could run I'd be going over the jumps at Hereford racecourse!"

A man went to the doctor and said, "I've just been playing rugby for the Luctonians and I felt fine but I got back home and I found that when I touched my legs, my arms, my head and everywhere else, it really hurt."

After a careful examination the doctor concluded, "You've broken your finger."

One night an old couple in Ross-on-Wye were lying in bed. The husband was falling asleep but the wife was in a romantic mood and wanted to talk.

She said, "You used to hold my hand when we were courting, my dear."

Wearily he reached across, held her hand for a second and tried to get back to sleep.

A few moments later she said, "Then you used to kiss me, my dear."

Mildly irritated, he reached across, gave her a peck on the cheek and settled down to sleep.

Thirty seconds later she said, "Then you used to nibble my neck, my dear."

Angrily, he threw back the bedclothes and got out of bed.

"Where are you going?" she asked.

"To get mi teeth!"

Q: What do you do when a Gloucester City fan throws a pin at you?

A: Run like mad, he's got a grenade in his mouth.

Three old boys, all a bit hard of hearing, were playing golf one fine day at the Kington Golf Club.

One remarked to the other, "Windy, isn't it?"

"No," the second man replied, "It's Thursday…"

"So am I," chimed in the third man, "Let's have a beer."

A pupil at a school in Hay-on-Wye asked his teacher, "Are 'trousers' singular or plural?"

The teacher replied, "They're singular on top and plural on the bottom."

A bloke walked up to the foreman of a road laying gang in Hereford and asked for a job. "I haven't got one for you today," said the foreman, looking up from his newspaper. "But if you walk half a mile down there, you'll find the gang and you can see if you like the work. I can put you on the list for tomorrow."

"That's great, mate," said the bloke as he wandered off down the road.

At the end of the shift, the man walked past the foreman and shouted, "Thanks, mate. See you in the morning."

The foreman looked up from his paper and called back, "You've enjoyed yourself then?"

"Yes, I have!" the bloke shouted, "But can I have a shovel or a pick to lean on like the rest of the gang tomorrow?"

Sam worked in a telephone marketing company in Kington. One day he walked into his boss's office and said, "I'll be honest with you, I know the economy isn't great, but I have three companies after me, and, with respect, I would like to ask for a pay rise."

After a few minutes of haggling, his manager finally agreed to a 5% pay rise, and Sam happily got up to leave.

"By the way," asked the boss as Sam went to the door, "which three companies are after you?"

"The electric company, the water company, and the phone company," Sam replied.

A police officer arrived at the scene of a major pile up on the A49.

The officer runs over to the front car and asks the driver, "Are you seriously hurt?"

The driver turns to the officer and says, "How should I know? Do I look like a lawyer?"

At the Farmers' arms pub in Wellington Heath, a newcomer asked a local man, "Have you lived here all your life?" The old man took a sip of his cider and, after a long pause, replied, "Don't know yet!"

At a doctor's surgery in Much Birch a patient was confiding in his G.P.

"Doctor, last night I made a Freudian slip. I was having dinner with my mother-in-law and wanted to say, 'Could you please pass the butter, ma.' But instead I said, 'You silly old cow, you've completely ruined my life and I can't stand the sight of your ugly mush'."

A jump-lead walks into a bar. The barman says, "I'll serve you, but don't start anything."

A farmer was driving along a country road near the picturesque village of Whistlefields with a large load of fertiliser. A little boy, playing in front of his cottage, saw him and called out, "What do you have on your truck?"

"Fertiliser," the farmer replied.

"What are you going to do with it?" asked the little boy.

"Put it on strawberries," answered the farmer.
"You ought to live here," the little boy advised him. "We put sugar and cream on ours."

It was a quiet night in Lugwardine and a man and his wife were fast asleep, when there was an unexpected knock on the door. The man looked at his alarm clock. It was half past three in the morning. "I'm not getting out of bed at this time," he thought and rolled over.

There was another louder knock.

"Aren't you going to answer that?" asked his wife irritably.

So the man dragged himself out of bed and went downstairs. He opened the door to find a strange man standing outside. It didn't take the homeowner long to realise the man was drunk. "Hi there," slurred the stranger. "Can you give me a push?" "No, I'm sorry I most certainly can't. It's half past three in the morning and I was in bed," said the man and he slammed the front door.

He went back up to bed and told his wife what happened. "That wasn't very nice of you," she said. "Remember that night we broke down in the pouring rain on the way to pick the kids up from the babysitter, and you had to knock on that man's door to get us started again? What would have happened if he'd told us to get lost?"

"But the man who just knocked on our door was absolutely sozzled," replied her husband.

"Well, we can at least help move his car somewhere safe and sort him out a taxi," said his wife. "He needs our help."

So the husband got out of bed again, got dressed, and went downstairs. He opened the door, but couldn't to see the stranger anywhere so he shouted, "Hey, do you still want a push?"

In answer, he heard a voice call out, "Yes please!"

So, still unable to see the stranger, he shouted, "Where are you?"
"I'm over here, mate," the stranger replied, "on your swing."

The president of the Ledbury Vegetarian Society really couldn't control himself any more. He simply had to try some pork, just to see what it tasted like. So one day he told his members he was going away for a short break. He left town and headed to a restaurant in Leominster. He sat down, ordered a roasted pig, and waited impatiently for his treat. After only a few minutes, he heard someone call his name, and, to his horror, he saw one of his members walking towards him. At exactly the same moment, the waiter arrived at his table, with a huge platter, holding a whole roasted pig with an apple in its mouth. "Isn't this place something?" said the president, thinking quickly, "Look at the way they serve apples!"

Phil's nephew came to him with a problem. "I have my choice of two women," he said, with a worried frown, "A beautiful, penniless young girl whom I love dearly, and a rich widow who I don't really love."

"Follow your heart," Phil counselled, "marry the girl you love."

"Very well, Uncle Phil," said the nephew, "That's sound advice. Thank you."

"You're welcome," replied Phil with a smile, "By the way, where does the widow live?"

At a school in Hereford, the maths teacher poses a question to little Lee, "If I give £500 to your dad on 12% interest per annum, what will I get back after two years."

"Nothing," says Lee.

"I am afraid you know nothing about maths, Lee," says the teacher crossly.

"I'm afraid too, sir," replies Lee, "You don't know nothing about me dad."

Did you hear about the fight in the chip shop last week? Six fish got battered!

A passenger in a taxi tapped the driver on the shoulder to ask him something.

The driver screamed, lost control of the cab, nearly hit a bus, drove up over the curb and stopped just inches from a large plate glass window.

For a few moments everything was silent in the cab, then the driver said, "Please, don't ever do that again. You scared the daylights out of me."

The passenger, who was also frightened, apologised and said he didn't realise that a tap on the shoulder could frighten him so much, to which the driver replied, "I'm sorry, it's really not your fault at all. Today is my first day driving a cab. I've been driving a hearse for the last twenty-five years."

A high-rise building was going up in Hereford and three steel erectors sat on a girder having their lunch.

"Oh, no, not cheese and pickle again," said Jim, the first one, "If I get the same again tomorrow, I'll jump off the girder."

Harry opened his packet. "Oh, no, not a chicken salad with mayo and lettuce on granary," he said. "If I get the same again tomorrow, I'll jump off too."

Owen, the third man, opened his lunch. "Oh, no, not another potato sandwich," he said. "If I get the same again tomorrow, I'll follow you two off the girder."

The next day, Jim got cheese and pickle. Without delay, he jumped. Harry saw he had chicken salad with mayo and lettuce on granary, and with a wild cry, he leapt too. Then the third man, Owen, opened his lunchbox. "Oh, no," he said. "Potato sandwiches." And he too jumped.

The foreman, who had overheard their conversation, reported what had happened, and the funerals were held together.

"If only I'd known," sobbed Jim's wife.

"If only he'd said," wailed Harry's wife.

"I don't understand it at all," said Owen's wife. "He always got his own sandwiches ready."

A farmer from in Gloucestershire once visited a farmer based near Clehonger in Herefordshire. The visitor asked, "How big is your farm?" to which the Herefordshire farmer replied, "Can you see those trees over there? That's the boundary of my farmland."

"Is that all?" said the Gloucestershire farmer, "It takes me three days to drive to the boundary of my farm."

The Clehonger man looked at him and said, "I had a car like that once."

The nervous young batsman playing for the Canon Frome Cricket Club was having a very bad day. In a quiet moment in the game, he muttered to the one of his team mates, "Well, I suppose you've seen worse players."

There was no response...so he said it again, "I said 'I guess you've seen worse players.'"

His team mate looked at him and answered, "I heard you the first time. I was just trying to think..."

There were two fish in a tank, one says, "You man the guns, I'll drive."

A young actor is very excited about appearing at the Market Theatre in Ledbury and can't wait to tell his father.

"Dad, guess what? I've just got my first part in a play. I play the role of a man who's been married for thirty years."

"Well, keep at it, son," replies his father, "Maybe one day you'll get a speaking part."

There's a man in Stroud who claims to have invented a game that's a bit like cricket; what he doesn't realise is Gloucestershire County Cricket Club's been playing it for years.

Did you hear about the truck driver from Gloucester who was seen desperately chiselling away at the brickwork after his lorry became stuck at the entrance to a tunnel? "Why don't you let some air out of your tyres?" asked a helpful passer-by.

"No, mate," replied the driver, "It's the roof that won't go under, not the wheels."

A man goes to his G.P. in Kingsland and says, "Doc, I can't stop singing *The Green Green Grass of Home*."

The doctor says, "That sounds like Tom Jones syndrome."

"Is it common?" asks the man.

"It's not unusual," the doctor replies.

A man walks into his G.P.'s surgery. He has a banana stuck in one of his ears, a potato in the other ear, and two carrots stuck up his nostrils.

The man says, "Doctor, this is terrible. What's wrong with me?" The doctor says, "Well, first of all, you need to learn to eat properly."

A man walks past a pet store in Leominster. There is a sign in the window that says TALKING DOG FOR SALE.

The man doesn't believe it, but he is curious so he goes into the store. He sees a Border Collie, walks up to the dog and says, "Alright, lad?"

The dog says, "Alright, mate. How are you?"

The man says "Blimey! You really can talk!"

The dog says, "That's right, mate."

The man says, "So what is it like being a talking dog?"

The dog says, "Well, I've lived a fine, full life. I rescued Avalanche victims in The Alps. I worked as a drug-sniffing dog for the FBI, and now I read to people in an old folks' home five days a week."

The man is absolutely amazed. He turns to the owner of the pet shop and says, "Hell's bells! Why would you sell a dog like this???"

The pet shop owner says, "Because he's a damn liar! He never did ANY of those things."

One day a Gloucestershire boy was in the back garden shouting, "Mum, why is my Gloucester City top lying on the grass?"

His Mum looked out the window and shouted,

"The thieving gits stole my pegs!"

A man and his wife walked past a swanky new restaurant in Ledbury. "Did you smell that food?" the woman asked. "Wonderful!"

Being the kind-hearted, generous man that he was, her husband thought, "What the hell, I'll treat her!" So they walked past it a second time.

Pete and Larry hadn't seen each other in many years. They were having a long chat, telling each other all about their lives. Finally Pete invited Larry to visit him in his new flat in Hereford. "I have a wife and three kids and I'd love to have you visit us." "Great. Where do you live?"

"Here's the address. There's plenty of parking behind the flat. Park and come around to the front door, kick it open with your foot, go to the lift and press the button with your left elbow, then enter! When you reach the sixth floor, go down the hall until you see my name on the door. Then press the doorbell with your right elbow and I'll let you in."

"Great. But tell me...what is all this business of kicking the front door open, then pressing elevator buttons with my right, then my left elbow?" Pete answered, "Surely you're not coming empty-handed?"

Many years ago there was a dispute between two villages, one in Herefordshire and the other in Gloucestershire. One day the villagers heard the cry, "One man from Herefordshire is stronger than one hundred Gloucestershire men."

The villagers in Gloucestershire were furious and immediately sent their hundred strongest men to engage with the enemy. They listened, horrified by the screams and shouts. After hours of fighting, all was quiet but none of the men returned.

Later on, the same voice shouted out, "Is that the best you can do?"

This fired up the people from Gloucestershire and they rallied round, getting a thousand men to do battle. After days of the most frightful blood-curdling sounds, one man emerged from the battlefield, barely able to speak, but with his last breath he managed to murmur, "It's a trap, there's two of them!"

A man's car stalls on a country road near the Forest of Dean. When he gets out to fix it, a horse in the nearby field comes up alongside the fence and leans over.

"Your trouble is probably in the injectors," says the horse.

Startled, the man jumps back and runs down the road until he meets a farmer. He tells the farmer his story.

"Was it a large white horse with a black mark over the right eye?" asks the farmer.

"Yes, yes." the agitated man replies.

"Oh, I wouldn't listen to her," says the farmer, "she doesn't know anything about cars."

Did you hear about the last wish of the henpecked husband of a house-proud wife?

He asked to have his ashes scattered on the carpet.

A hurrah Henry from Gloucestershire was driving around Leominster in his fancy new car and realised that he was lost. The driver stopped a local character, old Tom, and said, "Hey, you there! Old man, what happens if I turn left here?"

"Don't know, sir," replied Tom.

"Well, what if I turn right here - where will that take me?" continued the visitor.

"Don't know, sir," replied old Tom.

Becoming exasperated, the driver continued, "Well, what if I go straight on?"

A flicker of knowledge passed over old Tom's face but then he replied, "Don't know, sir."

"I say old man you don't know a lot do you?" retorted the posh bloke.

Old Tom looked at him and said, "I may not know a lot, sir, but I ain't lost like what you are!"
With that, old Tom walked off leaving the motorist stranded.

One day at the Hereford County Hospital, a group of primary school children were being given a tour. A nurse showed them the x-ray machines and asked them if they had ever had broke a bone.

One little boy raised his hand, "I did!"

"Did it hurt?" the nurse asked.

"No!" he replied.

"Wow, you must be a very brave boy!" said the nurse. "What did you break?"

"My sister's arm!"

Have you heard about the latest machine in the arcade in Hereford?

You put ten pence in and ask it any question and it gives you a true answer.

One visitor from Gloucester tried it last week.

He asked the machine "Where is my father?"

The machine replied:"Your father is fishing on the River Severn." "Well," he thought, "That's daft for a start because my father is dead."

Next he asked, "Where is my mother's husband?"
The reply came back, "Your mother's husband is buried in Stroud, but your father is still fishing on the River Severn."

Two blokes are standing in the Hereford Job Centre, waiting for their turn at the counter.

The first bloke says to the second one, "I have to buy my wife something nice for our wedding anniversary and the benefits cheque won't cover it."

The second bloke looks up from his paper and says, "What date?"

The first bloke thinks for a while and says, "15th September."

The second bloke considers his next question. "What year?"

Without taking a breath, the first bloke replies, "Every year for the last twenty-seven!"